SOME KIND OF CHRISTM

Cookies

Cakes

Pies

CANDY CANE

INGREDIENT

- White sugar: 1 kg
- Corn syrup: 300 ml
- Water: 70 ml
- Mint extract: 1/2 tsp
- Red food coloring
- White food coloring

MAKING

- Mix corn syrup, water in a deep pot with a capacity of about 2-3 liters.

- Add the sugar and stir, until the sugar has dissolved, continue to cook without stirring until the mixture reaches a temperature of 141 degrees Celsius, then remove the pan from the stove (to measure the temperature of the sugar, use a real thermometer). Products).

- Wait a little until the foam dissolves, then slowly add mint extract, stir well. Different types of peppermint oil can give different cake flavors. Because we can't taste sugar at such a high temperature, we will gradually adjust the amount of mint in the following batches and choose the most suitable one.

- Divide the mixture into 2 parts, 1 part pour on a baking tray and store in a hot oven to keep the candy in a liquid state. The remaining 1/2 you add a little red food coloring, stir well, you can add more, depending on whether you like pink or fiery red.

- Pour the mixture on a clean surface, wait a little for it to cool down, then use clean rubber gloves to pull the mixture into long fibers, pull and roll several times, then put the candy in a hot oven to keep it hot.

- Add the white food to the rest of the candy, repeat the same steps as with the red candy until you get a similar white candy bar.

- Take some red and white candies, twist them together, roll them to form a stick with two intertwined red and white colors.

- Bend the top of the candy to make it look like a cane, repeat with the rest of the pieces until all are gone.

- The last thing is to wait for the candy to cool completely, wrap it in a plastic bag and put it in a glass jar.

PECAN PIE

Pecan pie ingredients

- Pecans 250 gr
- All-purpose flour 272 gr
- Unsalted butter 170 gr
- 2 egg yolks
- Chicken eggs 3

- Corn syrup 246 gr
- Vanilla extract 1 tsp
- Sugar 200 gr
- 1 pinch salt
- Cold water 4 tbps

Implementation tools

Oven, whisk, sieve, mold, food wrap, stencils, rolling pin,...

How to make Pecan tart - pecan pie

1 Making the cake base

Sift 272g all-purpose flour and a pinch of salt into a bowl. Next, you add 142g of chopped unsalted butter, use your hands to squeeze the butter into the flour.

In another bowl, dissolve 4 tbps cold water and 2 egg yolks and pour into the bowl of flour, mix well.

Pour the mixture on the table, knead by hand until it forms a ball. Cover the dough with cling film and place in the refrigerator for 30 minutes.

2 Arrange the mold and bake for the 1st time
After it has cooled, transfer the dough to the table and roll the dough into a circle about 1/3 of a finger thick.

Place the dough in the round pan, use a knife or scissors to cut off the excess dough. To make the cake look more beautiful, use your hands to create a wavy shape for the edge of the cake.

Then, put a layer of parchment paper on the cake and then add about 500g of beans (optional) and spread evenly. This will help prevent the base of the cake from swelling when baking.

Place the cake base in the oven at 180 degrees Celsius for 15 minutes. Remember to preheat the oven for 15-20 minutes before baking so that the oven temperature is stable.

3 Make the filling and bake the 2nd time
Place 150g of pecans, 246g of corn syrup, 3 eggs, 200g of sugar, 28g of melted unsalted butter, 1 tsp of vanilla extract, 1/2 tsp of salt, and mix with a whisk.

When the base of the cake is done baking, take out all the beans and parchment paper, and pour the filling in the center of the cake. Next, arrange the remaining 100g of pecans on the cake to decorate it beautifully.

Finally, you put the cake in the oven for 20 minutes, then cover the cake with foil and bake for another 40 minutes until the cake is done.

4 Finished Products

The pecan pie after baking has a beautiful golden base, the pecans become darker. The crust is spongy, the inside is soft and moist, the pecans are fragrant, crispy and sweet.

CHOCOLATE PECAN PIE

Chocolate pecan pie ingredients

- Pecan nuts 175 gr
- All-purpose flour 200 gr
- Dark Chocolate 200 gr
- Unsalted butter 190 gr (cold)
- Chicken eggs 2

- Maple syrup 175 ml (maple syrup)
- Black sugar 100 gr
- Five-spice powder 1/8 tsp
- 1 pinch salt

Maple syrup

Maple syrup is produced from the sap of the sugar maple, red maple, or black maple.

This type of syrup has a texture that is slightly thick and similar to honey. It is often used to make cakes or sprinkle on desserts or marinate ingredients for baking and frying in food processing.

Implementation tools

Oven, bowl, spoon, knife, rolling pin, parchment paper, dough cutter, 23cm tart mold,...

How to make Chocolate pecan tart - chocolate pecan pie

1 Mix the dough for the cake base

First, put in a bowl 200g all-purpose flour, 100g cold unsalted butter, a little salt, and then use a dough cutter to mash the butter with flour.

Next, slowly add 2 tbps of ice cold water and quickly knead the dough with your hands until it forms a smooth, elastic mass.

Finally, compress the dough into a ball and cover with cling film, let the dough rest in the refrigerator for 15-20 minutes.

Pro tip: To keep the butter from melting, you should knead the dough quickly!

In case if the butter shows signs of melting, you must let the dough rest in the freezer for about 5 minutes before continuing to knead.

2 Arrange the mold and bake the cake base
Preheat oven to 180 degrees Celsius for 15 minutes.

After the dough hardens, take it out and then use a rolling pin so that the radius is about 3 inches larger than the mold.

Next, place the dough on the cake pan and press firmly with your hands to press the dough into the bottom and sides of the mold. Next, use a knife to cut off the excess dough and use a fork to tattoo evenly on the surface of the dough.

Small tip: To prevent the cake base from swelling and cracking when baking, remember to use a fork to tattoo the dough evenly!

Finally, cover 1 sheet of parchment paper on top of the dough, spread evenly with 1 layer of soybean seeds to insulate. Bake the first cake at 180 degrees C for 12 - 15 minutes.

Then, remove the parchment and bean layer and continue baking the second time for another 5 minutes.

Small tip: To prevent the cake from being scorched at the first baking stage, cover it with a layer of beans (soybeans, red beans, black beans, ...) or insulating balls!

3 Making chocolate fillings

Put in a bowl of 90g unsalted butter, 200g dark chocolate, then place this bowl over a pot of boiling water and stir until the mixture is completely melted and smooth.

In another bowl, add 100g of black sugar, 2 eggs, 175ml of maple syrup, 1/8 tsp of five-spice powder (optional) and stir well to combine.

Next, slowly add the chocolate butter mixture to the egg bowl, stirring constantly until the mixture is smooth.

4 Arrange the filling and bake the cake for the 2nd time

Arrange 1/2 of the pecans on the cake base, then pour all the chocolate filling into the mold. Then, continue to decorate the remaining pecans dial and bake the cake at 180 degrees C for 35 minutes.

5 Finished Products

Chocolate pecans tart has a golden crust, fragrant buttery nose.

The cake when bitten into has a standard crunchy texture mixed with the bitter sweetness from the chocolate filling, the pecans are crispy, the fatty flesh is extremely delicious and extremely nutritious.

CHRISTMAS TREE CAKE

Ingredients

- All-purpose flour 213 gr
- Sugar 200 gr
- Baking soda 1 gr
- Baking powder 3 gr

- 3 eggs
- Sour cream 120 gr
- Fresh milk 120 ml
- Mint extract 1/2 tsp
- Butter 630 gr
- Vanilla extract 20 ml
- Ice cream cone shell 12 pieces
- Green food coloring 5 ml
- Powdered sugar 850 gr

Implementation tools
- Oven, whisk, bowl, cake mold 15cm

How to make Christmas tree cake

1 Mix cake batter

Put 213g flour, 1/4 tsp salt, 3g baking powder and 200g sugar in a bowl and mix well.

2 Mix butter and egg mixture

Add 120g of sour cream, 120ml of fresh milk and 176g of melted butter.

Next, add the whites of 3 eggs and 20ml of vanilla extract and mix well.

3 Molding

Prepare 3 15cm cake molds, use a spray bottle to spray one layer each or you can replace the anti-stick spray oil with wax paper, a non-stick mold or use a mixture of butter and flour to spread around the cake mold.

Then, add the egg butter mixture to the cake flour mixture and stir well. Finally, divide the dough evenly into 3 15cm molds.

4 Baking

Turn on the oven at 177 degrees Celsius and then put the cake molds in the oven and bake for 30 minutes at 177 degrees Celsius.

5 Cut the waffles

Use a knife to cut the waffle half lengthwise and the waffle half across

6 Make buttercream

Add 454g of butter and 1/2 tsp of salt and stir until loose. Then, add 850g of powdered sugar, 1/2 tsp of mint extract and keep stirring

7 Decorate the cake

Add 5ml of green food coloring to 1/2 of the buttercream to create a green color.

After that, draw 2 white and green spirals on the surface of the baked cake, then stack another cake and continue drawing in the same way.

Next, spread the white buttercream over the stack of cakes and smooth the surrounding cream with the top.

Using a waffle cut in half, spread green buttercream around and decorate like a pine tree on the top of the cake.

Finally, cut the waffle in half lengthwise, cover with green buttercream on the surrounding surface and decorate evenly on the side of the cake, then sprinkle powdered sugar over the cake to create a snow shape.

8 Finished Products

Christmas tree cake has a sweet, delicious taste combined with an eye-catching Christmas atmosphere. This is a must-have in winter.

SANTA CLAUS CUPCAKES

Ingredients for Santa Claus Cupcakes

- Wheat flour 180 gr
- Cocoa powder 33 gr
- Powdered sugar 1 kg
- Peanut butter 0.5 kg

- Baking powder 3 gr
- Baking soda 9 gr
- Sour cream 59 ml
- Fresh milk with sugar 118 ml
- Chicken eggs 2
- Salt 2.8 gr
- 2ml vanilla essence
- Vegetable oil 79 ml
- 1/2 lemon
- Food coloring 2 ml
- Decorative candies 30 gr

Implementation tools
- Oven, whisk, whisk, sieve,...

How to make Santa Claus Cupcakes

1 Sift flour mixture

Sift 180 grams of flour, 266 grams of powdered sugar, 3 grams of baking powder, 9 grams of baking soda, 2.8 grams of salt, and 33 grams of cocoa powder into a mixing bowl. Then use a spatula to mix.

Tip: You can sifted about 2-3 times to make the flour mixture smooth, without lumps.

2 Mix the egg mixture

Put in a bowl 79ml vegetable oil, 118ml fresh milk with sugar, 2 eggs, 2ml vanilla essence, 59ml sour cream and squeeze 1/2 lemon into it. Use a whisk to beat the eggs until smooth.

Next, slowly pour 60ml of hot coffee into the egg mixture. You just pour the coffee while stirring the mixture.

3 Mix cake dough

Pour the egg mixture into the previous bowl. Use a mixer or whisk to mix well, forming a homogeneous mixture.

4 Molding and baking

Preheat oven to 170 degrees Celsius for 15 minutes to stabilize oven temperature.

Line a cupcake mold with parchment paper and place 1/2 of the dough in the pan. Then, put the cake in the oven for 30 minutes at 177 degrees Celsius.

5 Whip the buttercream

Place in mixing bowl 0.45kg peanut butter at room temperature. Turn on the mixer on medium speed until the butter is smooth and creamy.

Next, sift about 0.75kg of powdered sugar into the mixing bowl. Continue to use the machine to mix well and add 2ml of vanilla essence, mix until the mixture is fluffy and smooth.

Finally divide the mixture into 3 parts. One part, you put a little red food color in the ice cream, mix well. The second part, you use the heart tree to dip a little pink in, mix well for the cream to be evenly colored. The rest you put in the ice cream bag.

Tip: You can divide the sugar into 3 parts and then sift each part in, mixing well to make the mixture smoother.

6 Decorate Santa Claus

Spread light pink icing on the center of the cake. Next, spread the red cream on top to create a hat-like shape. Add chocolate candies to create eyes and nose

Then, spray some whipped cream on the empty cake to create a beard for Santa and add a little more on the hat as shown below.

7 Finished Products

The cupcakes with Santa Claus are both lovely and eye-catching. Each piece of cupcake is soft, spongy and lightly fragrant with the smell of coffee and the fatty taste of eggs. Avocado ice cream has a moderate sweetness so when you eat it, you will not feel bored at all.

CHRISTMAS GINGERBREAD

Material

- 200g all-purpose flour
- Baking powder: tsp
- 2 tsps ginger powder
- Cinnamon powder: tsp
- An egg white

- Unsalted Butter: 80g
- Powdered sugar: 150g
- Brown sugar: 50g
- Honey: 50ml
- Salt: tsp
- vanilla tube
- 1 tsp lemon juice

Doing

Step 1 Add flour, ginger powder, cinnamon powder, salt and mix well. Then sift the flour mixture until smooth, and place in a large bowl.

Step 2 Put the butter in the microwave until melted. Add the sugar to the butter and beat until combined. Then add the eggs, continue beating until the mixture is smooth. Then add vanilla powder and honey and beat well.

The dough should form a smooth, flexible mass. If the dough is still doughy, add a little more flour to the mixture or put the dough in the fridge to dry before rolling it out.

Step 3: Roll the dough and shape it

Put a little dry flour on the rolling tray to prevent the dough from sticking. Roll the dough to about 3mm thin. If you have a cake mold available, you just need to press down to have a cake with a beautiful shape.

If a cake mold is not available, you can use a sharp knife to shape and cut the cake.

Step 4: Bake the cake

Place a sheet of parchment paper on top of the baking sheet and place the rolled pieces on top. Preheat oven to 180 degrees and bake for about 15 minutes until golden brown.

If you want to preserve the cake longer or want the cake to be more crispy, you can leave the cake in the oven for a few more minutes at 100 degrees. Remember to carefully observe to check, don't leave it for too long, it will burn.

Step 5: Decorate the cake

After taking the cake out of the oven, let it cool before decorating.

You beat the egg whites until fluffy, then add the lemon juice and beat in small numbers.

Put the beaten egg in the ice cream bag and then draw a decoration on the cake, maybe add a little color to enhance the taste. Place the decorated cake in the oven to dry at 100 degrees Celsius for 1 minute.

So finished the delicious Christmas gingerbread batch. Hopefully with the Christmas cake recipe with a fairly simple recipe, the whole family's Christmas party will add more flavor.

Also you can make gingerbread house with the same implementation. Just cut the molds of the house and put them together. Then use the decorative cream on top to have a snow-white house for Christmas.

BUCHE DE NOEL

Baking material

- Fresh milk without sugar 40 ml (warmed)
- Unsalted butter 15g (melted)
- Cooking oil 25g (reheated)
- Wheat flour 25 g

- Cocoa powder 25 g
- Chicken eggs 4 eggs
- Sugar 80 g
- Cream of tartar 1/2 tsp
- Whipping cream 150 ml
- Dark chocolate 150g (topping)
- G butter n 15 nuts (cream frosting)
- Whipping cream hot 150 ml (topping)

Tools: Christmas decorations placed on the cake, oven, stencils, cake molds, egg beaters, ...

How to make Christmas tree cake - Buche de noel

1 Make a sponge cake

Whisk together milk, cooking oil and butter in a large bowl. Then, sift the flour and cocoa powder into the mix, then add 4 egg yolks and mix to combine.

Beat 4 egg whites with 80g of sugar and 1/2 tsp of cream of tartar (can be substituted with lemon juice).

Mix the egg whites one at a time into the flour mixture, remember to mix gently by hand to avoid bursting air bubbles in the whites leading to poor baking.

Place the dough into a baking sheet lined with parchment paper and bake at 170 degrees Celsius for 20-30 minutes.

When the cake is done, take out the cake and roll it quickly into a clean towel to keep the cake sticky.

2 Shape the cake

Whip 150 ml of whipping cream and spread over the cake. Then roll up and refrigerate for about 30 minutes.

Heat 150 ml whipping cream. In a large bowl add 150 g of bitter chocolate and 15 g of unsalted butter. Slowly pour the hot whipping cream into the bowl to melt the chocolate.

Cut 2 slices of cake to make a log shape. Spread this chocolate on the cake and decorate as you like.

3 Finished Products

Enjoying the fragrant, soft, sweet chocolate-flavored log cakes during Christmas is really nothing like. Let's show off your kitchen skills to make this indispensable dessert for your Christmas dinner. Good luck!

APPLE PIE

Ingredients to be prepared

– Wheat flour: 500g

– Eggs: 1 egg

– Unsalted butter: 10g

– Fresh milk: 200ml

- Water

- Apples: 6 apples
- Salted coffee: 1 tbsp
- White granulated sugar: 1/3 cup
- Red sugar: 1/3 cup
- Lemon juice: 2 tsps
- Nutmeg powder: spoon
- Cinnamon powder: 1 tsp
- Cooking oil
- Pie mold: 18cm

How to do it step by step

1. Kneading the Dough for Baked Apple Pie Crust

Step 1: In a large bowl add flour, salt, and fresh milk. The butter is cut into pieces, then put in a bowl and knead the dough by hand.

Step 2: Crack the eggs into the bowl and add a little bit of filtered water.

Continue kneading until the flour mixture comes together to form a ball. When doing this step, do not add too much water at the beginning if the dough will be difficult to knead.

In the process of kneading the dough, you can add a little more dry flour if the dough is too sticky, but do not add too much flour as it will make the cake dry.

Step 3: After the dough has been kneaded, it becomes smooth and smooth, we cover the dough with wax paper or plastic wrap tightly.

Put the dough mixture in the refrigerator for about 45-90 minutes until the dough is flexible enough to perform the rolling process.

2. Roll the Dough for Baked Apple Pie Crust

Step 4: After the dough is finished, we will perform the rolling step. Take 2/3 of the dough in the mixture, spread the dough on a flat surface and then roll the dough. The dough is rolled into a circle about 3mm thick.

- Step 5: Gently place the rolled dough into the apple pie mold, then cut off the excess dough to make it beautiful. Roll the remaining 1/3 of the dough into a circle, the diameter of this dough is equal to the cake mold to make the cake surface.

- Step 6: Cover the cake mold with 1/3 of the rolled dough, then put the cake mold in the refrigerator for another 30 minutes to let the dough rest.

3. How to Make Baked Apple Pie Filling

– Step 7: Red apples are washed, peeled and cut into equally beautiful pomegranate seeds, then put in a bowl. Add white sugar, red sugar, lemon juice, nutmeg powder, cinnamon powder and a little salt to mix well.

4. How to Bake Baked Apple Pie

– Step 8: Take out the crust from the refrigerator, put the filling inside without leaving any leftovers. Brush an extra layer of oil around the crust that protrudes around the edge of the cake pan.

– Step 9: Cut the remaining round dough into arbitrary 0.8-1cm wide strips of dough to decorate the cake.

Can be arranged in a basket weave or spokes on the face of the mold to make the cake more beautiful. In addition, you can use cookie cutters to cut into stars, hearts, etc. to replace the basket spokes.

– Step 10: Bake the cake in the oven at 190 degrees Celsius, cook until the cake is cooked and then enjoy.

CHRISTMAS TREE CUPCAKES

Ingredients

- For the cake:
- A glass of oil
- A cup of soured cream
- ¾ A cup of cream

- 4 eggs
- 1 box of cake dough chocolate
- Optional 1 tsp espresso powder

- For enamel:
- Cool 2 cups butter and press
- 10 cups granulated sugar
- 2 tbps vanilla
- Cup plus 2 tbps thick cream
- A little salt, Additional elements:
- Green gel food product
- Tips for pipes 1 m
- Candy bag, Scattering of golden stars
- Festive distribution

Instructions

How to prepare a cake:
Thunderstorms possible, warmth 515 ° F. Cover the cake tin with a cupcake liner.

Mix the oil, vanilla, sour cream, thick cream and eggs by hand or with a mixer. Then mix the packaged cake mixture, chocolate and espresso powder if using.

Place the dough on the cake pan shape, i favor to use ¼ measuring cups.

Bake for quarter-hour or until the inserted toothpaste is clean. make sure to bake all the cakes within the oven on the identical shelf in order that they bake evenly.

Refrigerate the cake for five minutes, then place on a shelf to chill. Freeze the cake until completely cooled. How to make ice (this is my standard vanilla cream double recipe):

In a blender, whisk the butter pieces over medium-high heat until the butter is light and fluffy.

Add 1 cup of granulated sugar

Once the granulated sugar becomes hard to feature, add the vanilla, thick cream and a pinch of salt to mix the ingredients completely.

Add the green gel coloring until you get the required greens.

OATMEAL CHOCOLATE COOKIES

Ingredients for chocolate oatmeal cookies

- 200g all-purpose flour
- 90 grams of unsweetened cocoa powder, sifted
- 1/2 tsp baking soda
- 1/2 tsp table salt
- 1/2 tsp cinnamon powder

- 230 grams of unsalted butter, cut into pieces
- 1 tbsp of water
- 250 grams of brown sugar
- 250 grams of bitter chocolate, chopped
- 2 large eggs
- 130 grams of oatmeal

Oatmeal Chocolate Cookie Maker

- Clean bowl
- Wooden spoon
- Double water bath (Steamed)
- Baking tray
- Stencils
- Oven mitts
- Ice cream scoop
- Cake cooling rack (Bracket)

How to make chocolate oatmeal cookies

Step 1:

– Preheat oven to 180 degrees Celsius.

– Place parchment paper on a baking tray. Set aside.

Step 2:

In a small bowl, mix all-purpose flour, unsweetened cocoa powder, baking soda, table salt, cinnamon powder, and oats together. Set aside.

In a double pot, add the unsalted butter, bitter chocolate, brown sugar, and water to the top of the pot. With the pot below, pour a little water to bring it to a boil. The water will evaporate and melt the butter and chocolate. Use a wooden spoon to stir occasionally.

Note: When the mixture becomes smooth, they still have a little grain that is not smoothed by the brown sugar!

Step 3:
- Turn off the stove. Add eggs and beat well. Finally, add the dry flour mixture on top and beat well once more. The mixture will be in a thick consistency.

– Use an ice cream scoop and scoop each cake onto the baking tray lined with parchment paper you prepared in advance. Each cake is spaced 2 to 3 cm apart. Do this until you run out of cakes.

Step 4:
Place the cake in the oven and bake for about 12 minutes. At this point, the cake will only be slightly soft in the middle, turn the baking tray halfway. Let cool for about 5 minutes before placing the cake on the cake cooler and the cake will cool completely.

– So you have joined us in the kitchen and learned how to make delicious chocolate oatmeal cookies! The cake will be delicious and attractive if you eat it with a glass of hot milk! It's great, isn't it?

JEWELED COCONUT DROPS

Ingredients

- 1/3 cup butter
- 3 ounces cream cheese
- 3/4 cup sugar
- 1 large yellow, room temperature
- 2 tbps orange juice
- 1 tsp almond extract

- 1-1/4 cup all-purpose flour
- Baking powder 1-1/2 tsp
- 1/4 tsp salt
- 3-3/4 cup sweet grated coconut, sliced
- 1 cup seedless raspberries, heated

Guide

Cream butter, cream cheese, and sugar until fluffy and light. Mix egg yolks, orange juice, and almond extract. In a separate bowl, mix flour, baking powder and salt together with a whisk.

Beat gradually into the cream mixture. Add 3 cups of coconut and stir well. Refrigerate for about 30 minutes until easy to handle.

Preheat oven to 350°. Put a spoonful of flour in a bowl. The remaining coconut roll. Enter 2. It is placed on a top plate that does not unfold.

Using the tip of a wooden spoon handle, press deep indentations in the center of each one. Bake for 8-10 minutes until edges are lightly browned. Let cool for 1 minute. Use a wooden spoon to open up grooves that may shrink or close. Remove cookies from pan to wire rack. Full of preservatives; completely cold.

CHOCOLATE PEPPERMINT SNAPS

Element

- 2 chocolate chips half every week, divided
- 1 large egg, at temperature
- 1 cup sugar, divided
- 1/2 cup vegetable oil
- 1/4 cup syrup

- 1 tbsp mint extract
- 1 tsp flavourer
- 2 cups universal flour
- 1 tsp sodium hydrogen carbonate
- 1/4 tsp salt
- 1/3 cup raw chopped mint

Directions

Preheat the oven to 350 °. Melt 1 cup of chocolate chips within the microwave. Stir until smooth; It's cold. In another bowl, beat eggs, 2/3 cup sugar, butter, syrup and extract until well combined.

Melt in chocolate. during a separate bowl, mix the flour, saleratus and salt. Whisk within the mint mixture. Fold within the remaining candy and chocolate chips.

Put the remaining sugar in an exceedingly shallow bowl. Roll out the dough to 1 inch. ball; rolling on the road. Enter 2. Spread on a baking sheet lined with paper. Bake until the highest is broken and therefore the cake is prepared, 12-15 minutes. Let cool within the pan for 1 minute before removing until cool.

PEPPERMINT PUFF PASTRY STICKS

Element

1 sheet of frozen puff pastry, thawed

1-1 / 2 cups chopped mint

10 ounces milk chocolate caramel coating, finely chopped

Direction

Preheat the oven to 400 °. Open the pastry sheet. 2 Cut in half to form a rectangle. Cut each rectangle horizontally into 18 strips about 1/2 inch wide. Place in oil paste. Cook until golden brown, 12-15 minutes. Remove the wire from the pan to the grill to cool completely.

Place the chopped candies in a shallow bowl. Melt the caramel coating in the microwave. Stir until smooth. Dip one half into each cookie. allow excessive leakage. Sprinkle with mint candies. Put on wax paper; Wait until installation. Store in a sealed container.

CHOCOLATE CRINKLE COOKIES

The components

2 cups dark chocolate, separated

2 tbps butter, softened

1 cup sugar

2 large egg whites at temperature

1-1/2 tsps flavoring

1-1/2 cups all-purpose flour

1-1/2 tsps leavening

1/4 tsp salt

1/4 cup water

1/2 cup confectioner's sugar

Direction

Melt 1 cup of chocolate chips within the microwave. Stir until smooth. set aside. Beat butter and sugar until golden brown, about 2 minutes. Add egg whites and vanilla. good hit. Stir within the melted chocolate.

In another bowl, whisk together flour, leaven and salt. Gradually add within the butter mixture, alternating with the water. Mix the remaining chocolate pieces. Place in refrigerator, covered, about 2 hours until easy to handle.

Preheat oven to 350°. Form the dough into 1 in. balls. appear confectioner's sugar. Place 2 inches on top of every other on a baking sheet coated with cooking spray. Bake until cakes rise, 10-12 minutes. Remove to wire rack to chill.

CHOCOLATE TRICKS

Although chocolate chip cookies are very simple to create, there are some small ways in which can get it wrong confirm your leaven isn't stale, or it won't be as fresh. Butter shouldn't be too soft - half-hour on the counter should be enough.

And confirm your cookie sheets are clean, cool, and slot in the oven. Here are some reasons why your cookies can be flat.

What makes a cookie wrinkled?

The cookie crumbs are so cute and this level of loveliness is achieved by starting the baking process with the cookie dough into balls rather than squeezing it flat because the dough heats up and sets, it deflates into an ideal cookie and cracks appear.

The contrast of chocolate powder and granulated sugar makes this chocolate chip cookie recipe so beautiful. See the last word guide to differing kinds of cookies.

Freshly baked cookies will be stored at temperature in an airtight container for 4 to five days. Alternatively, you'll be able to freeze baked cookies during a single layer, or separate with parchment paper, for 3 to four weeks.

Chocolate crumbs are often shaped into balls and left to solidify in an exceedingly single layer on a baking tray. Once frozen, store them in an airtight container within the freezer for 3 months. When you're able to bake, let it defrost for half-hour, add the cake sugar, and bake as directed.

Add texture to the classic chocolate chip cookies by stirring during a cup of chopped dried cherries or a cup of chocolate chips (white, milk, or black). Add a bit festive flavor, including 1 tsp mint extract and 1/2 cup mint or crushed sugar cane. For an espresso, replace the water with strong (cold) coffee.

LEMON SNOWFLAKES

Ingredients

1 packet of mixed lemon (standard size)

2-1 / 4 cup whipped cover

1 large egg, temperature

sugar cane

Drection

Heat the oven to 350 °. Stir the prepared mixture, boiled cream and eggs in a large bowl until well combined. The dough is very sticky.

Pour sugar in each tbsp. Cover gently with a shirt. Place the unleavened bread on a baking sheet. Cook for 10-12 minutes until golden brown and crisp. Go to the side to cool.

FESTIVE THUMBPRINTS

Attach

- 1 cup butter, softened
- 1/2 cup sugar
- 1 large egg, temperature
- 1 tsp seasoner
- 2 cups multipurpose flour

- 1/4 tsp salt
- Sprayed or unprepared paint
- to complete: .
- 1 cup sugar
- 1/4 cup butter, diced
- 1/4 cup 2% milk
- 8 ounce white candy topping
- 1 tsp flavourer
- red, green food product

Rules

Preheat the oven to 350 °. Lightly coat with oil and cream until golden and milky. Add egg and vanilla. Mix the flour and salt during a bowl; gradually boost the cream mixture.

Put the spoons in an exceedingly shallow plate or bowl. Roll out the dough into balls of balls; spraying the mountains.

Place 2 on a baking sheet. Use your finger to press the inner text between each of them. Bake for 10-12 minutes until the perimeters are soft. Use the handle of a wooden spoon to centre or out. Remove the wire from the plate to cool down.

For the filling, mix the sugar, butter and milk in an exceedingly small saucepan, stirring constantly. Cook for 1 minute, then stir. Remove from the burner.

Add sweetener and vanilla; blend until smooth. Divide the filling between 2 cups. Fill one container with red foodstuff and also the other with green foodstuff. Spoon filling notch; you have got to attend until it's determined.

CHOCOLATE CANDY CANE COOKIES

Ingredients for making Chocolate Candy Cane Cookies

- Candy cane 100 gr (crushed)
- All-purpose flour 125 gr
- Cocoa powder 60 gr
- Baking soda 3 gr

- Crushed chocolate 170 gr (optional)
- Dark Chocolate 120 gr (60% cocoa)
- Unsalted Butter 113 gr
- 2 eggs
- Sugar 200 gr
- Salt 3 gr
- 3ml mint essence

How to make Chocolate Candy Cane Cookies

1 Melt butter and chocolate

Place 120g of dark chocolate and 113g of unsalted butter in a glass bowl, place in a pot of boiling water, then heat in a water bath over medium heat.

Use a spatula to stir the mixture quickly and evenly. Then take it down and let it cool.

2 Beat eggs

In a bowl, beat 2 eggs with 120g of sugar.

Use an electric mixer to beat the mixture until light froth, many small bubbles appear, then add 3ml of mint extract and melted chocolate mixture. Continue beating the mixture until combined.

3 Mix dry powder

In another bowl, sift 125 grams of flour, 3 grams of baking soda and 3 grams of salt, and then mix with a whisk.

4 Mix the cake mix

Add half of the dry powder mixture to the chocolate mixture that has just been beaten in step 2, use a flat spatula to gently mix until the powder dissolves.

Continue to add the remaining half of the flour and 60g of cocoa powder, mix well until the flour mixture is combined.

Finally, add 170g of chocolate chips, stir well to finish the cake mixture.

Pro tip: Breaking up the flour mixture makes it easier to mix and the cake mix to homogenize faster.

5 Baking

Preheat the oven to 165 degrees Celsius before baking for 15-20 minutes. Use an ice cream scoop to scoop the dough into a tray lined with baking paper, spaced about 5cm apart.

Place candy cane crumbs on the dough balls. Then put the cake tray in the oven and bake at 165 degrees Celsius for 10-15 minutes until the cake is fully baked.

Pro tip: During the baking process, you should use a light-colored (except black) baking tray, which will transfer heat better and help the cake to burn less.

6 Finished Products

Once the cake is done, take it out of the oven and let it cool. While the cake is still warm, you can place more candy cane crumbs on top of the cake.

Chocolate candy cane cookies with the aroma of butter, the bitter taste of chocolate and beautiful colors from candy cane are so attractive and unique, aren't they? Let's go to the kitchen and make it right now!

SNOWFLAKE COOKIES

Snowflake-shaped sugar cookies ingredients

- Flour No. 8 375 gr
- Unsalted Butter 230 gr
- Sand sugar 200 gr
- Powdered sugar 290 gr
- 1 chicken egg

- Fresh milk 4 tbps (or water)
- Baking soda 1/2 tsp (Baking soda)
- Salt 1/2 tsp
- Vanilla essence 12 ml

Implementation tools

Barrel oven, egg beater, cage stirrer, snowflake-shaped stainless steel mold, stencils, ice cream bag, rolling mat,...

How to make snowflake-shaped sugar cookies

1 Beat butter and sugar

You put 230g of unsalted butter and 200g of granulated sugar in a bowl, then beat with a whisk until the sugar and butter are melted.

Next, you add 1 egg, 10ml of vanilla essence (about 2 tsps) into a bowl and continue to beat for about 3-5 minutes to blend.

2 Sift flour

Sift 375g of flour, 1/2 tsp of salt, and 1/2 tsp of baking soda into the butter-sugar mixture.

Then use an electric mixer to beat the flour mixture until there are no lumps. To make the dough more smooth, continue to use a flat spatula to mix well. Next, let the dough rest for 30 minutes.

3 Molding and baking

After the dough rests, place the dough on the rolling mat and then use a rolling pin to spread the dough about 1/4 inch thick.

Place the dough on a rolling mat and roll until the dough is about 1/4 knuckle thick.

Use a snowflake shaped stainless steel mold to emphasize the entire dough to shape the cake, gently place the cake on a baking tray lined with parchment paper.

Note: Arrange the cake evenly on the tray about 1/2 inch apart so that the cake is cooked evenly and does not stick together.

Next, put the cake tray in the refrigerator for 30 minutes to stand the dough, when baking, it keeps its original shape.

Turn on the oven before 5-10 minutes to preheat the oven, then bake the cake for 10-12 minutes at a temperature of 180 degrees Celsius. When the cake is done, take it out and let it cool.

4 Coloring the line

You add 290g of powdered sugar, 4 tbps of milk (or water), 2ml of vanilla essential oil (about 1/4 tsp), use a spatula to mix until the mixture is smooth.

Pro tip: If the mixture is too thick, add more milk (or water), if too liquid add more sugar.

Next you prepare 2 ice cream bags with small round tails.

Put 1/2 of the sugar mixture into the ice cream bag, the rest in the bowl, add a little purple food color to create color when decorating, use a spatula to beat the color evenly and then put it in the remaining ice cream bag.

Note: Do not add a lot of food coloring because the candy will be bitter.

You can also color food with fruit to ensure health safety.

See more: How to make simple and safe food coloring with natural ingredients

5 Decoration

You use a bag of uncolored sugar to draw a thin line around the cake, then use a purple bag of sugar to cover a thin layer inside the border.

Next, use a bag of colorless sugar to draw diagonal lines on the surface to create a snowflake shape. You can also decorate according to your own preferences.

6 Finished Products

When finished, sugar cookies will have a snowflake shape with eye-catching colors, when eaten, the candy layer has a sweet taste without bitterness, the layer of cookies is golden, crispy, with the scent of butter and the fatty taste of eggs.

SPARKLING CRANBERRY WHITE CHOCOLATE CAKE

Ingredients

- Small blueberries
- 2 cups fresh cranberries
- 1 1/2 cups (310 g) of sugar, divide
- 1 glass of water (240 ml).
- Blueberry pie

- 3 1/3 cup (433 g) all-purpose flour
- 2 cups sugar (414 g).
- Baking powder 2 1/2 tsps
- 1 1/2 cups (336 g) butter, salt (340 g), temperature
- 3 eggs
- 2 tbps vanilla
- 1 cup (240 ml) cream
- 1 cup milk (240 ml).
- 3 cups fresh cranberries

- White chocolate fish
- 12 ounces chocolate
- 3/4 cup (180 ml) cream
- 3/4 cup (168 g) butter at temperature
- 8-9 cups (920-1035 g) granulated sugar

Recommended

Blueberry:

1. Boil 1 cup of sugar and water in boiling water. Cook until the sugar is totally dissolved.
2. Pour plain syrup into a heat-resistant bowl and let cool for 10 minutes.
3. Add the cranberries and blend until smooth.
4. Put the frozen cranberries within the syrup overnight, stirring some times to form the syrup.
5. Remove the cranberries from the syrup and grind with the remaining 1/2 cup sugar. you've got to roll some times to possess some layers of sugar on top.
6. Let the cranberries dry for about an hour.

Blueberry Cake:

1. Preheat the oven to 350 degrees. Prepare three 8-inch cake trays and coat the underside of the tray with saleratus and parchment paper.

2. Mix flour, sugar and leavening in a very large bowl.

3. Add butter, eggs, seasoning, cream and milk and beat on medium speed until smooth. don't overmix.

4. Gently mix within the cranberries.

5. Spread the dough between the three cakes.

Bake for 35-40 minutes, until the toothpaste with a bit powder is added.

7. Refrigerate for 10 minutes, then place on a wire rack to cool down completely.

White Chocolate Fish:

1. Put the chocolate in a very metal bowl.

2. microwave the cream until it boils. Remove from the microwave and pour within the chocolate chips.

3. Cover the bowl with wrapping for 5-7 minutes.

4. Beat the chocolate and cream until smooth.

5. Let the ganache sit until it's mostly cool. It should be thick.

6. Beat the tamarind with a blender for 2-3 minutes, until well combined and puffed.

7. Add butter and blend well.

Gently add the granulated sugar and beat until well combined. Add more cream if needed.

Include the cake:

1. Use an outsized serrated knife to get rid of the dome cake from the cake.

2. Place the primary layer of cake within the cake pan. Spread the frosting evenly on top.

3. Add the second layer of cake and evenly add more frosting on top.

4. Spread the last layer of cake on top and freeze the surface of the cake.

5. Cover the cake with shiny cranberries, adding a bit to the perimeters if desired.

Note

I think most cakes are best left a minimum of 12-24 hours after icing. Let the taste fall. This cake is moist for some days after icing.

CHRISTMAS LIGHT CUPCAKES

Apparatus

- Cup of cake
- Mix 1 box of milk
- 1 small box of pudding mixture
- teeth 3
- 3/4 cup vegetable oil

- 1/2 cup water, 3/4 cup cream
- 2 tbps flavorer
- Decoration:
- vanilla cream
- Black Frost bought in stores

Suggestions

Preheat oven to 350 °. Fill two muffin bags with 18 pieces of paper.
Add cupcake ingredients to a lightweight bowl. Shake well, for about 3 minutes, stirring occasionally.

Divide the flour evenly between the muffin pans. Bake for 18 to 22 minutes, or until the toothpaste comes out clean. Let it cool completely.

Using a large kitchen utensil, roll the butter cream into the cakes. Draw a black line around Frost ground. Attach the M & Ms vertically to the edges of the cakes

COOKIE CHOCOLATE CHIP

Ingredient

- 165 grams unsalted butter (approx. 3/4 cup unsalted butter)
- 80 grams white sugar (1/4 cup plus 3 Tbsp caster sugar)
- 80 grams brown sugar (1/4 cup plus 2 Tbsp brown sugar)
- 2 egg yolks (18 – 20 grams/yolk) – refrigerated

- 2 tsps vanilla extract (2 tsp vanilla extract)
- 300 grams all-purpose flour (2 cups plus 4 Tbsp all-purpose flour)
- 1/2 tsp baking soda (1/2 tsp baking soda/bicarb)
- 1/4 tsp table salt (1/4 tsp salt)
- 130~150 grams chocolate chips

Making

1. Melt the butter and then let it cool to harden and form a paste and slightly mushy.

2. Add white sugar and yellow sugar and mix well with butter. When the butter and sugar are just combined, add the eggs and vanilla and mix well.

3. Sift flour, baking soda, and salt into another bowl, mix well. Preheat oven to 190 °C (two fires).

4. Divide the dough into 3 parts. Sift each part into the bowl of butter and sugar, mix well. Place about 4/5 of the chocolate chips in a bowl and mix well.

5. Divide the dough into about 30 grams, and place on a tray lined with baking paper. Each dough ball should be spaced about 3-5 cm apart.

* If the dough is too pasty and sticky, difficult to shape, you can put the dough in the refrigerator for about 20 to 30 minutes to harden the dough, it will be easier to shape the cake.

6. Shape the dough into a round ball and then press the dough down slightly. When baking melted butter, the dough will spread out on its own to form a circle.

7. Use 1/5 of the remaining chocolate chips to stick around the cake balls. After baking, the chocolate will remain on the cake, making the cake more beautiful.

8. Baking:

* If you want the cake to be crispy from the inside out: Bake at 190 °C for about 12 minutes. After 8 - 9 minutes, when the cake is slightly golden, turn the tray upside down, bake for another 3 minutes until the edges are slightly golden brown. Take the cake out, leave on the tray for 5 minutes and then transfer to a rack to cool completely.

* If you want the cake to be crispy on the outside but soft on the inside: Bake at 170 degrees Celsius for about 15 minutes. After 10-12 minutes, when the cake turns slightly golden, turn the tray upside down, bake more until the edges are slightly golden brown. Take the cake out, leave on the tray for 5 minutes and then transfer to a rack to cool completely.

9. Store the cake in an airtight container, can add a desiccant bag. Use for 1-2 weeks. If the cake is mushy or not crispy enough, turn on the oven at 110 degrees Celsius, put the cake into the oven again for 5-8 minutes (don't leave it for too long, it will harden).

COOKIE HEART LINZER

Ingredients for sweet heart linzer cookies

- 2 cups flour
- 1 cup cornstarch
- 1/4 tsp salt
- 3 sticks of butter, soft
- 1 cup of sugar

- 1 egg

- 1 tsp pure vanilla

- 2 cups roasted, peeled, and chopped chestnuts

- 6 ounces bitter chocolate, finely chopped

- 1/2 cup seedless raspberry jam

- 1/2 cup Sugar (for sifting)

Making

Step 1. Sift flour, cornstarch, and salt into a medium bowl.

Step 2. In a large bowl, beat butter and sugar with an electric mixer, mixing on high speed until well combined, about 1 minute is best. Whisk together egg and vanilla, toss with mixture, scraping sides of bowl as needed. With mixer on low speed, mix in flour mixture, just until even. Mix in the chestnuts and chocolate.

Step 3. Cover the dough and put it in the fridge for at least 2 hours. Then, use a rolling pin to roll the dough to about 1/4 inch thick. Use a 3 1/2 inch heart mold to cut the dough and shape it. You should cut the dough as close as possible to avoid excess dough.

Step 4. Preheat oven to 325 degrees.

Only 4 simple steps, the heart-shaped cookie is finished, it will be a special gift for the other half to surprise!

HOLIDAY ALMOND TASSIES

Ingredients

- 1 cup butter, good
- 6 ounces cheese, good
- 2 cups multi-function flour
- Charging:
- 2 cans (8 ounces each) to put almonds

- 2 cups sugar
- large eggs, normal temperature, beaten slightly.
- tbps fruit crush
- tbps thick cream
- 1 tsp of flour for various purposes
- 1/4 cup chopped almonds

Instructions

In a large bowl, mix the butter and cheese until light and crispy. Slowly add the flour and stir well. Ball shape 48. along with your fingers dipped in flour, press the underside and top edges of atiny low greasy muffin cup

In a large bowl, mix almond paste, sugar, eggs, fruit crush, cream and flour to fill. Fill in three -quarters of the finished page. Sprinkle with almonds.

Bake at 400 degrees until golden brown, 12-13 minutes. Cool on a wire rack for 10 minutes before carefully removing from the pan to chill completely.

PUDDING COOKIES WITH SPRINKLES

Ingredients:

- Butter and Shortening - i prefer to use a mix of butter and shortening for this recipe.
- granulated sugar
- Mayai

- Vanilla Extract - Use 100% pure flavouring for best taste.
- Flour for all purposes
- Vanilla Pudding Blend — 3.4 ounces box of instant vanilla blend. ensure you don't catch the cook serving the pudding my fault, it's not right and it doesn't work for this recipe.
- Baking powder
- Salt
- Christmas Springs - We use a mix of red, green and white like this one, but you'll use any color you wish.

Instruction

Step 1: Preheat the oven to 350°F. Line two baking sheets with parchment paper or silicone baking mats and put aside.

Step 2: employing a stand mixer or hand mixer in a very large bowl, cream with butter, shortening, and sugar until light and smooth (4-5 minutes).

Step 3: Quickly beat eggs, vanilla and pudding mixture.

Mix in an exceedingly large bowl with an electrical mixer with the sugar and sugar coated butter and also the pudding mixture, eggs, and seasoning is added.

Step 4 In another bowl, combine the flour, leaven and salt. Slowly add the butter mixture, a bit at a time, mixing between additions.

A hand-held mixer within the corner of an oversized bowl with the butter mixture and dry ingredients is added little by little.

Step 5: Place the spray in an exceedingly small shallow bowl. employing a kitchen utensil or table spoon, roll out the cookie dough and roll it in your hands to create a ball.

Place the flour balls in a very spray bowl and roll to put them within the spray. Place on prepared cooking utensil, about 2 inches apart.

Step 6: Bake for 12-15 minutes or until lightly browned at the perimeters. Allow the cookies to chill on the cooking utensil for five minutes, then move to a cool rack to chill completely

CHRISTMAS GOOEY BUTTER COOKIES

As an ingredient

- 1/2 cup unsalted butter, grind
- 1 (8 ounce) packet of cheese, grind
- 1 egg

- 1 tsp flavourer
- 1 mixture for cake
- Scatter the cup, divide
- A cup of candy sugar

Suggestions

Mix cream with butter and cheese. Add eggs and vanilla and blend until combined. Beat until the cake is soft. Add a cup of sprinkles. Refrigerate for a minimum of 1 hour or overnight.

Preheat oven to 350 degrees. Remove the pan or rows with parchment paper. Remove the round tbps from the dough and roll into 1-inch balls. Sprinkle the ball with icing and appear sugar until completely covered.

Place about 2 inches on the prepared baking sheet. Bake for 8-10 minutes, then place on a baking sheet for 2 minutes, then transfer to a wire rack until completely coolol

CHRISTMAS TREE COOKIE STACKS

Required items

- Cookies
- 3/4 c. Butter without butter at temperature
- 1 c. Sugar
- 1 egg
- 1 tbsp seasoner

- 1 tbsp almond juice
- 2 1/4 c. Flour is beneficial for all
- 1 tbsp sodium bicarbonate
- 1/4 tsp. Coke salt

- Snow
- 1 c. Avocado
- 4 c. granulated sugar
- 1 tbsp flavouring
- 3 tbsp. Water or milk
- Green Jelly icing color
- 3 tbsp. Sprinkle with red and white pearls
- 18 Shoot the yellow star

Directions

Preheat the oven to 350 and place two sheets of cookies on parchment paper.

Add the soured cream and sugar together for 3 to 4 minutes until light and soft. Combine eggs and vanilla with almond juice. during a separate bowl, mix the dry ingredients together. Put the dry ingredients in a very bowl and blend until smooth. The flour are superb.

Make cookies in three sizes: 1 tbsp, 2 tbps and three tbps. (Each should be variety two.) Place an oversized center cookie on the cookware and press each slightly. Bake for 7 to eight minutes, until well cooked through. Add a bit flour to a different cooking utensil and press lightly. Bake for five to six minutes.

When the cookies are ready, remove from the oven and let cool for two to three minutes, then transfer to a cookie rack to chill completely.

Cool: Beat butter until soft. Add half the granulated sugar and blend until smooth. Add the vanilla and two tbps of water and blend until smooth. Add the remaining granulated sugar and blend until smooth. Apply icing blue gel on the snow and blend until you get the shade of green you would like.

Combine cookies: Get one size for every cookie. Fill the bag with the medium-sized star tube end (I used Wilton 32) and fill the bag with snow blue.

Place the frozen dessert on the biggest cookie and add the second middle cookie on top of it. Put the frozen dessert within the second cookie and place on top of alittle cookie. Sprinkle with star-shaped air tube and circular garnish on the ultimate cookie. Continue making cookies and refrigerate until able to serve.

CHRISTMAS CAKE

Material

- All-purpose flour: 100g
- Cornstarch: 40g
- 4 chicken eggs
- Light Butter: 3g
- Fresh milk without sugar: 30ml

- Vanilla: 5ml
- Sugar: 100g
- Half a tsp of salt
- 1 little cooking oil
- 200 ml Whipping Cream
- Lemon: 10ml

Doing

Step 1: Make the sponge cake

Separate the egg whites, use a whisk to beat the egg whites.

When large air bubbles appear, add lemon juice and salt and continue to beat vigorously. When these air bubbles are reduced, add sugar and continue to beat until the cake is fluffy.

Add vanilla and fresh milk to the remaining egg yolks. Beat the mixture until smooth and combined.

Use a sieve to finely sift the all-purpose flour and cornstarch into the egg yolks and mix well. Add the beaten egg whites to the egg yolk mixture. Mix well by hand, avoid doing it for too long, it will cause the cake to be called.

Put the cake mixture into the mold, remember to brush the oil on the cake pan so that the cake does not stick. Pre-heat the oven for 10 minutes at 150 degrees, then put the cake in and bake for about half an hour, until the cake is cooked.

Prepare the mold, lined with parchment paper to prevent the cake from sticking. Preheat oven to 175 degrees Celsius. Once the cake is done, take it out of the oven to cool.

Use a cookie cutter to make a house shape. That's it, you have the cake core right away to make an easy-to-make Christmas cake.

Step 2: Make the icing to decorate the cake

Put Whipping Cream in a bowl and beat with a whisk. Hit in one direction, at medium speed. Lift up the beater stick, if it doesn't stick to the stick, it will form a pyramid.

Step 3: Decorate and finish

Put the cream in the ice cream bag. Make a pyramid according to the edge of the house or decorate it according to your liking.

Add colorful candies to make the house more lively.

With just the above steps, you have an easy and simple Christmas cake for Christmas. In addition to the house cake, the Christmas tree cake is also an option for you.

HOT CHOCOLATE

Ingredient

- 250g pure chocolate
- 1 liter of fresh milk without sugar
- White diameter, few grains of fine salt
- 100ml whipping cream
- A little cinnamon powder

- Christmas canes, marshmallows, gingerbread, etc. (optional)

How to make hot chocolate

Step 1: Chop the chocolate into small pieces so that when the chocolate melts, it melts faster and there are no lumps. Place the chocolate in a glass or stainless steel bowl, put it in a pot of water, and simmer over low heat until the chocolate slowly melts. Or heat in the microwave on high for 2-3 minutes.

Step 2: When the chocolate has melted, add unsweetened milk, add sugar and a little salt according to taste. Continue to simmer until warm milk evaporates, then add whipping cream, stir quickly to mix well and turn off the heat. You can add chocolate if you like it more bitter or add whipping cream if you like it more fatty.

Step 3: Take a glove or a glove to lift the chocolate bowl and pour the hot chocolate into the cup. Add a little cinnamon powder to enhance the flavor of the mixture, you can skip this step if you don't like the taste of cinnamon.

Step 4: Decorate the cup of hot chocolate with gingerbread, Christmas canes and add a few marshmallows to enjoy right away.

CONTENTS

Candy cane 4

Pecan pie 8

Chocolate pecan pie 13

Christmas tree cake 20

Santa Claus cupcakes 26

Christmas gingerbread 32

Buche de noel 37

Apple pie 41

Christmas Tree Cupcakes 47

Oatmeal chocolate cookies 51

Jeweled Coconut Drops 56

Chocolate Peppermint Snaps 59

Peppermint Puff Pastry Sticks 62

Chocolate Crinkle Cookies 64

Lemon Snowflakes 69

Festive Thumbprints 71

Chocolate candy cane cookies 74

Snowflake cookies 79

Sparkling Cranberry White Chocolate Cake 86

Christmas Light Cupcakes 92

Cookie chocolate chip 94

Cookie heart linzer 99

Holiday Almond Tassies 102

PUDDING COOKIES WITH SPRINKLES 105

Christmas Gooey Butter Cookies.. 109

Christmas Tree Cookie Stacks... 112

Christmas cake 116

Hot Chocolate 120

Printed in Great Britain
by Amazon